A Little Book

– of –

Scottish
Quotations

Compiled By
J D Sutherland

Appletree Press

First published in 1997 by
The Appletree Press Ltd, 19-21 Alfred Street,
Belfast, BT2 8DL.

Tel: ++44 (0) 1232 243074
Fax: ++44 (0) 1232 246756

A Little Book of Scottish Quotations

A catalogue record for this book
is available from The British Library.

ISBN 0-86281-678-5

9 8 7 6 5 4 3 2 1

~ Contents ~

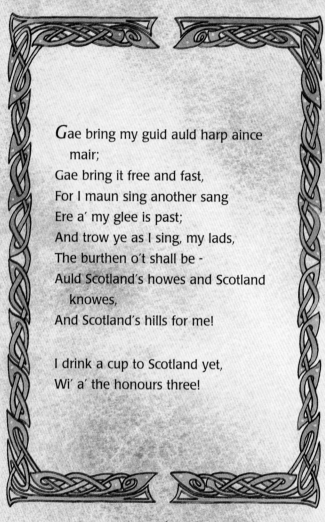

Gae bring my guid auld harp aince
    mair;
Gae bring it free and fast,
For I maun sing another sang
Ere a' my glee is past;
And trow ye as I sing, my lads,
The burthen o't shall be -
Auld Scotland's howes and Scotland
    knowes,
And Scotland's hills for me!

I drink a cup to Scotland yet,
Wi' a' the honours three!

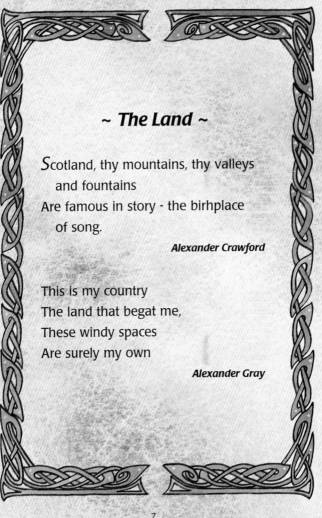

~ *The Land* ~

Scotland, thy mountains, thy valleys
   and fountains
Are famous in story - the birhplace
   of song.

Alexander Crawford

This is my country
The land that begat me,
These windy spaces
Are surely my own

Alexander Gray

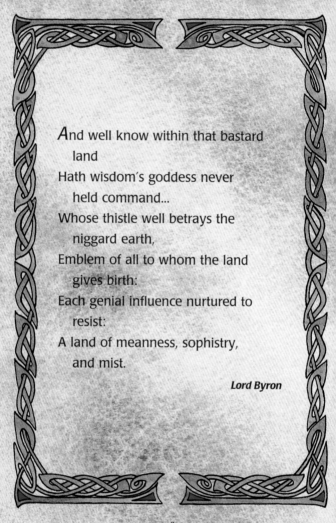

And well know within that bastard
    land
Hath wisdom's goddess never
    held command...
Whose thistle well betrays the
    niggard earth,
Emblem of all to whom the land
    gives birth:
Each genial influence nurtured to
    resist:
A land of meanness, sophistry,
    and mist.

Lord Byron

8

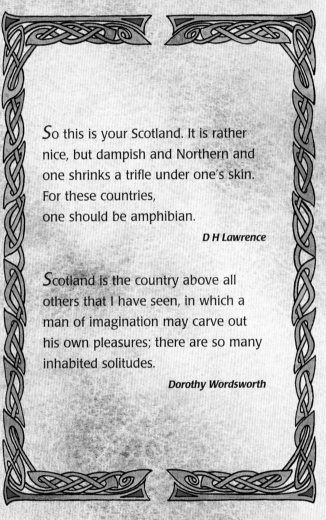

So this is your Scotland. It is rather
nice, but dampish and Northern and
one shrinks a trifle under one's skin.
For these countries,
one should be amphibian.

D H Lawrence

Scotland is the country above all
others that I have seen, in which a
man of imagination may carve out
his own pleasures; there are so many
inhabited solitudes.

Dorothy Wordsworth

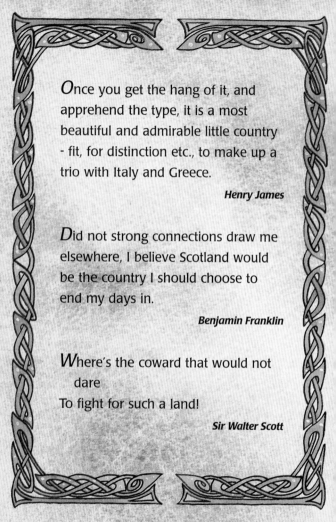

*O*nce you get the hang of it, and apprehend the type, it is a most beautiful and admirable little country - fit, for distinction etc., to make up a trio with Italy and Greece.

Henry James

*D*id not strong connections draw me elsewhere, I believe Scotland would be the country I should choose to end my days in.

Benjamin Franklin

*W*here's the coward that would not dare
To fight for such a land!

Sir Walter Scott

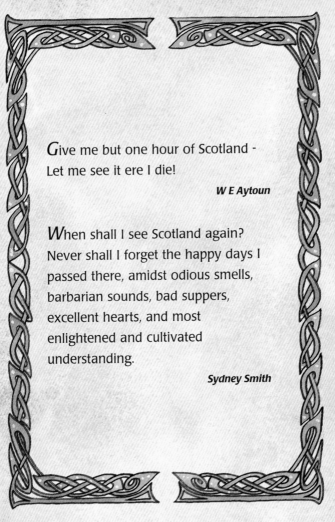

Give me but one hour of Scotland -
Let me see it ere I die!

W E Aytoun

When shall I see Scotland again?
Never shall I forget the happy days I
passed there, amidst odious smells,
barbarian sounds, bad suppers,
excellent hearts, and most
enlightened and cultivated
understanding.

Sydney Smith

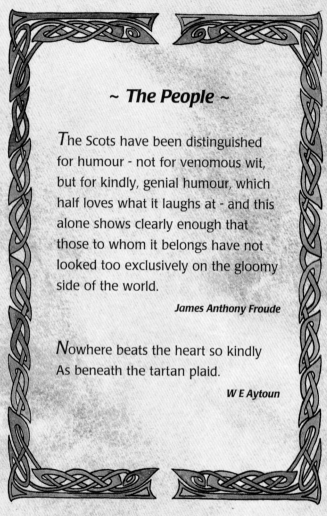

~ *The People* ~

The Scots have been distinguished
for humour - not for venomous wit,
but for kindly, genial humour, which
half loves what it laughs at - and this
alone shows clearly enough that
those to whom it belongs have not
looked too exclusively on the gloomy
side of the world.

James Anthony Froude

Nowhere beats the heart so kindly
As beneath the tartan plaid.

W E Aytoun

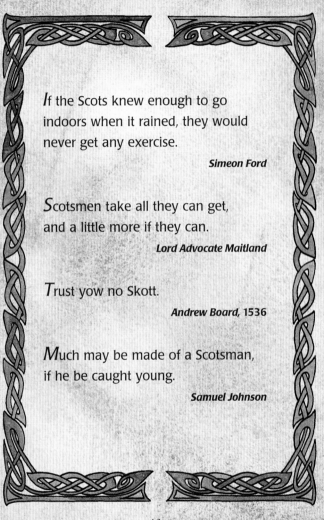

If the Scots knew enough to go indoors when it rained, they would never get any exercise.

Simeon Ford

Scotsmen take all they can get, and a little more if they can.

Lord Advocate Maitland

Trust yow no Skott.

Andrew Board, 1536

Much may be made of a Scotsman, if he be caught young.

Samuel Johnson

13

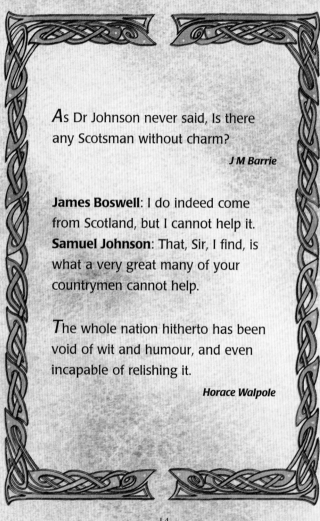

As Dr Johnson never said, Is there any Scotsman without charm?

J M Barrie

James Boswell: I do indeed come from Scotland, but I cannot help it.
Samuel Johnson: That, Sir, I find, is what a very great many of your countrymen cannot help.

The whole nation hitherto has been void of wit and humour, and even incapable of relishing it.

Horace Walpole

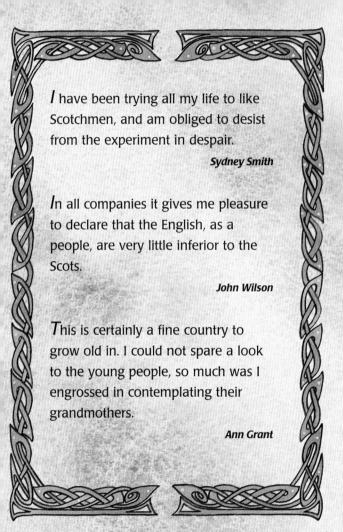

I have been trying all my life to like Scotchmen, and am obliged to desist from the experiment in despair.

Sydney Smith

*I*n all companies it gives me pleasure to declare that the English, as a people, are very little inferior to the Scots.

John Wilson

*T*his is certainly a fine country to grow old in. I could not spare a look to the young people, so much was I engrossed in contemplating their grandmothers.

Ann Grant

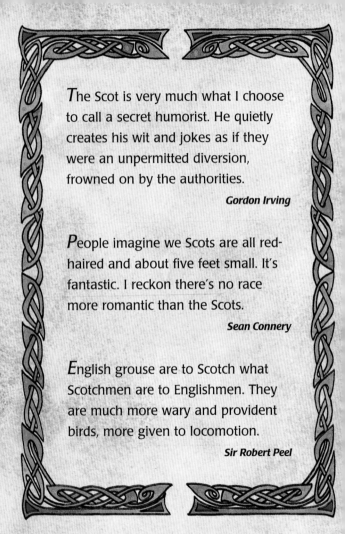

*T*he Scot is very much what I choose to call a secret humorist. He quietly creates his wit and jokes as if they were an unpermitted diversion, frowned on by the authorities.

Gordon Irving

*P*eople imagine we Scots are all red-haired and about five feet small. It's fantastic. I reckon there's no race more romantic than the Scots.

Sean Connery

*E*nglish grouse are to Scotch what Scotchmen are to Englishmen. They are much more wary and provident birds, more given to locomotion.

Sir Robert Peel

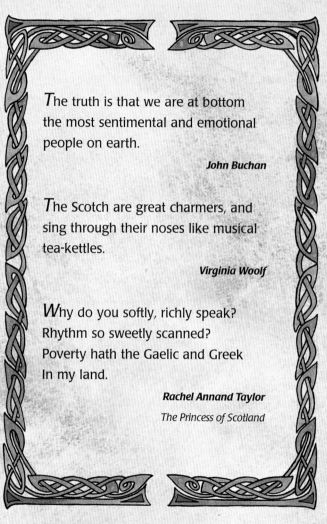

*T*he truth is that we are at bottom
the most sentimental and emotional
people on earth.

John Buchan

*T*he Scotch are great charmers, and
sing through their noses like musical
tea-kettles.

Virginia Woolf

*W*hy do you softly, richly speak?
Rhythm so sweetly scanned?
Poverty hath the Gaelic and Greek
In my land.

Rachel Annand Taylor
The Princess of Scotland

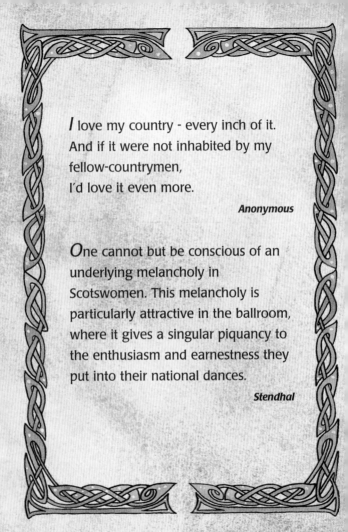

I love my country - every inch of it.
And if it were not inhabited by my
fellow-countrymen,
I'd love it even more.

Anonymous

*O*ne cannot but be conscious of an
underlying melancholy in
Scotswomen. This melancholy is
particularly attractive in the ballroom,
where it gives a singular piquancy to
the enthusiasm and earnestness they
put into their national dances.

Stendhal

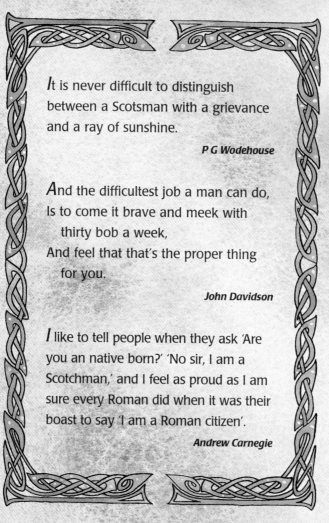

It is never difficult to distinguish between a Scotsman with a grievance and a ray of sunshine.

P G Wodehouse

And the difficultest job a man can do,
Is to come it brave and meek with
    thirty bob a week,
And feel that that's the proper thing
    for you.

John Davidson

I like to tell people when they ask 'Are you an native born?' 'No sir, I am a Scotchman,' and I feel as proud as I am sure every Roman did when it was their boast to say 'I am a Roman citizen'.

Andrew Carnegie

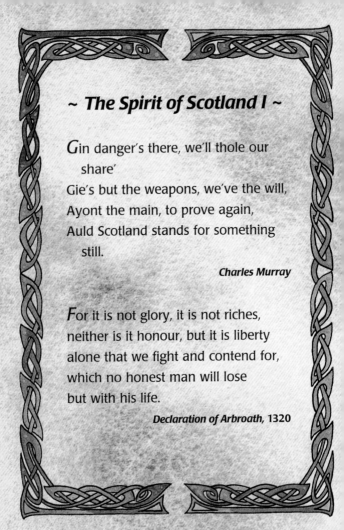

~ *The Spirit of Scotland I* ~

Gin danger's there, we'll thole our
   share'
Gie's but the weapons, we've the will,
Ayont the main, to prove again,
Auld Scotland stands for something
   still.

Charles Murray

For it is not glory, it is not riches,
neither is it honour, but it is liberty
alone that we fight and contend for,
which no honest man will lose
but with his life.

Declaration of Arbroath, 1320

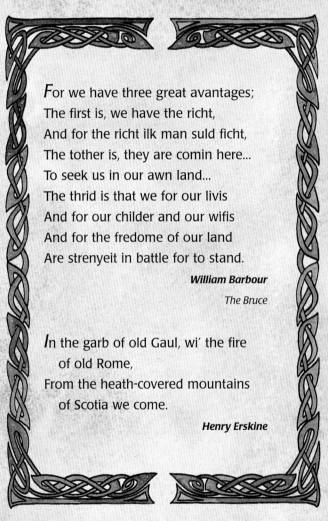

*F*or we have three great avantages;
The first is, we have the richt,
And for the richt ilk man suld ficht,
The tother is, they are comin here...
To seek us in our awn land...
The thrid is that we for our livis
And for our childer and our wifis
And for the fredome of our land
Are strenyeit in battle for to stand.

William Barbour

The Bruce

*I*n the garb of old Gaul, wi' the fire
   of old Rome,
From the heath-covered mountains
   of Scotia we come.

Henry Erskine

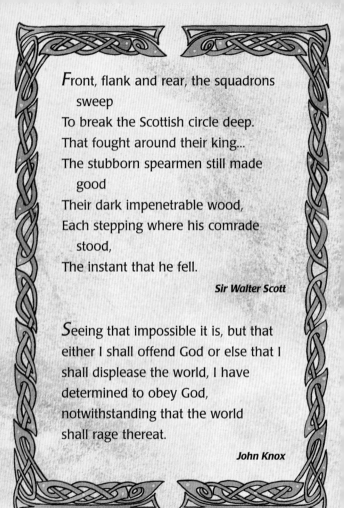

_F_ront, flank and rear, the squadrons
   sweep
To break the Scottish circle deep.
That fought around their king...
The stubborn spearmen still made
   good
Their dark impenetrable wood,
Each stepping where his comrade
   stood,
The instant that he fell.

Sir Walter Scott

_S_eeing that impossible it is, but that
either I shall offend God or else that I
shall displease the world, I have
determined to obey God,
notwithstanding that the world
shall rage thereat.

John Knox

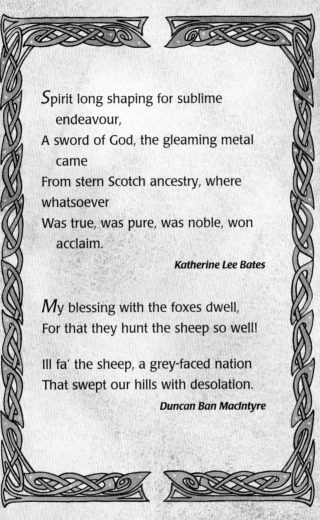

Spirit long shaping for sublime
   endeavour,
A sword of God, the gleaming metal
   came
From stern Scotch ancestry, where
whatsoever
Was true, was pure, was noble, won
   acclaim.

Katherine Lee Bates

My blessing with the foxes dwell,
For that they hunt the sheep so well!

Ill fa' the sheep, a grey-faced nation
That swept our hills with desolation.

Duncan Ban MacIntyre

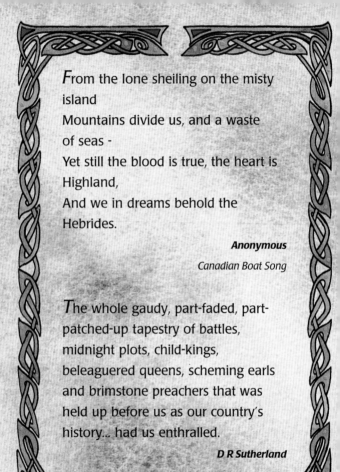

*F*rom the lone sheiling on the misty
island
Mountains divide us, and a waste
of seas -
Yet still the blood is true, the heart is
Highland,
And we in dreams behold the
Hebrides.

Anonymous

Canadian Boat Song

*T*he whole gaudy, part-faded, part-
patched-up tapestry of battles,
midnight plots, child-kings,
beleaguered queens, scheming earls
and brimstone preachers that was
held up before us as our country's
history... had us enthralled.

D R Sutherland

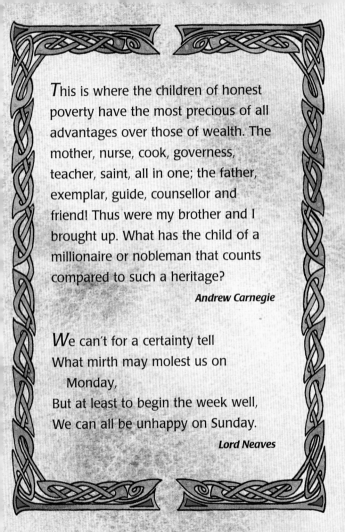

This is where the children of honest poverty have the most precious of all advantages over those of wealth. The mother, nurse, cook, governess, teacher, saint, all in one; the father, exemplar, guide, counsellor and friend! Thus were my brother and I brought up. What has the child of a millionaire or nobleman that counts compared to such a heritage?

Andrew Carnegie

We can't for a certainty tell
What mirth may molest us on
   Monday,
But at least to begin the week well,
We can all be unhappy on Sunday.

Lord Neaves

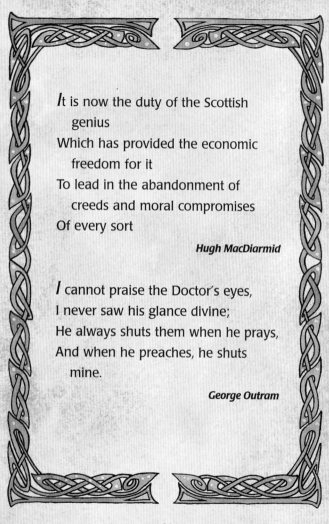

It is now the duty of the Scottish
  genius
Which has provided the economic
  freedom for it
To lead in the abandonment of
  creeds and moral compromises
Of every sort

Hugh MacDiarmid

I cannot praise the Doctor's eyes,
I never saw his glance divine;
He always shuts them when he prays,
And when he preaches, he shuts
  mine.

George Outram

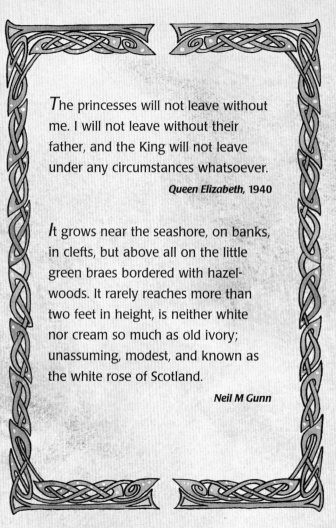

*T*he princesses will not leave without me. I will not leave without their father, and the King will not leave under any circumstances whatsoever.

Queen Elizabeth, 1940

*I*t grows near the seashore, on banks, in clefts, but above all on the little green braes bordered with hazel-woods. It rarely reaches more than two feet in height, is neither white nor cream so much as old ivory; unassuming, modest, and known as the white rose of Scotland.

Neil M Gunn

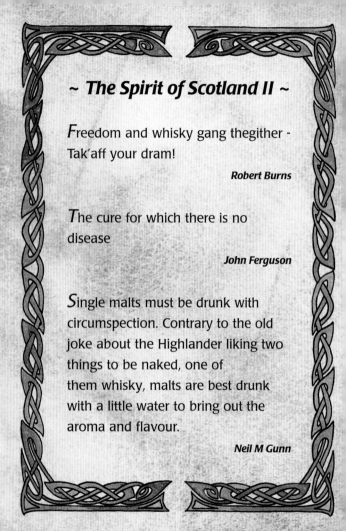

~ *The Spirit of Scotland II* ~

*F*reedom and whisky gang thegither -
Tak'aff your dram!

Robert Burns

*T*he cure for which there is no
disease

John Ferguson

*S*ingle malts must be drunk with
circumspection. Contrary to the old
joke about the Highlander liking two
things to be naked, one of
them whisky, malts are best drunk
with a little water to bring out the
aroma and flavour.

Neil M Gunn

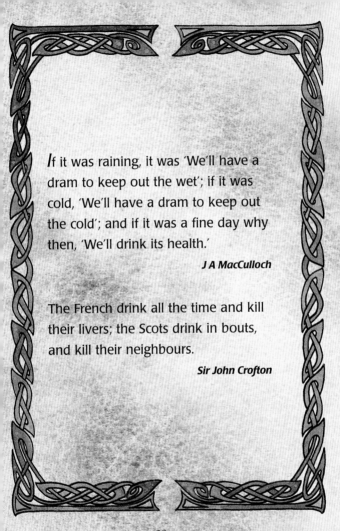

*I*f it was raining, it was 'We'll have a dram to keep out the wet'; if it was cold, 'We'll have a dram to keep out the cold'; and if it was a fine day why then, 'We'll drink its health.'

J A MacCulloch

The French drink all the time and kill their livers; the Scots drink in bouts, and kill their neighbours.

Sir John Crofton

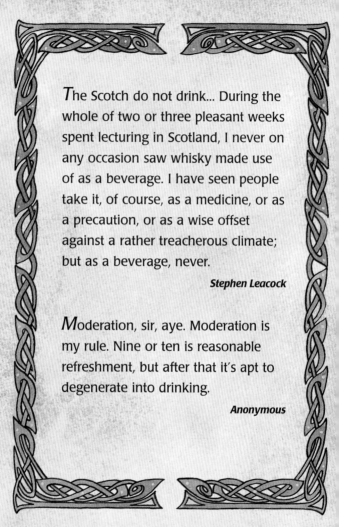

*T*he Scotch do not drink... During the whole of two or three pleasant weeks spent lecturing in Scotland, I never on any occasion saw whisky made use of as a beverage. I have seen people take it, of course, as a medicine, or as a precaution, or as a wise offset against a rather treacherous climate; but as a beverage, never.

Stephen Leacock

*M*oderation, sir, aye. Moderation is my rule. Nine or ten is reasonable refreshment, but after that it's apt to degenerate into drinking.

Anonymous

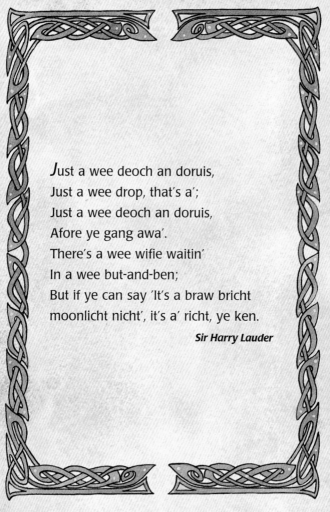

Just a wee deoch an doruis,
Just a wee drop, that's a';
Just a wee deoch an doruis,
Afore ye gang awa'.
There's a wee wifie waitin'
In a wee but-and-ben;
But if ye can say 'It's a braw bricht
moonlicht nicht', it's a' richt, ye ken.

Sir Harry Lauder

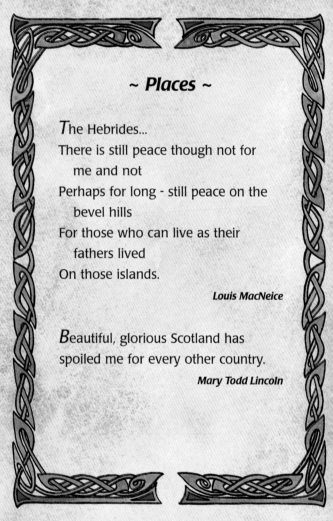

~ *Places* ~

The Hebrides...
There is still peace though not for
    me and not
Perhaps for long - still peace on the
    bevel hills
For those who can live as their
    fathers lived
On those islands.

Louis MacNeice

Beautiful, glorious Scotland has
spoiled me for every other country.

Mary Todd Lincoln

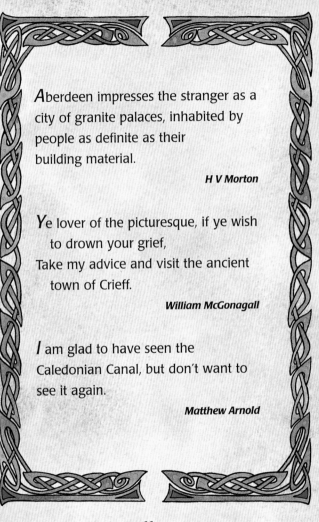

*A*berdeen impresses the stranger as a city of granite palaces, inhabited by people as definite as their building material.

H V Morton

*Y*e lover of the picturesque, if ye wish
   to drown your grief,
Take my advice and visit the ancient
   town of Crieff.

William McGonagall

I am glad to have seen the Caledonian Canal, but don't want to see it again.

Matthew Arnold

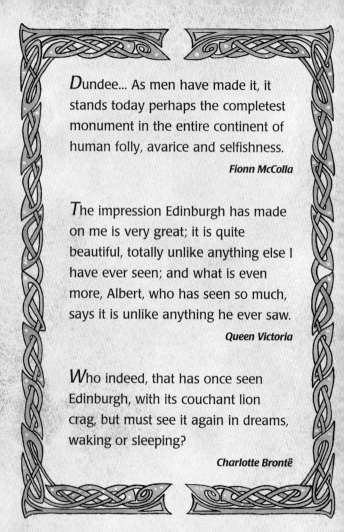

*D*undee... As men have made it, it stands today perhaps the completest monument in the entire continent of human folly, avarice and selfishness.

Fionn McColla

*T*he impression Edinburgh has made on me is very great; it is quite beautiful, totally unlike anything else I have ever seen; and what is even more, Albert, who has seen so much, says it is unlike anything he ever saw.

Queen Victoria

*W*ho indeed, that has once seen Edinburgh, with its couchant lion crag, but must see it again in dreams, waking or sleeping?

Charlotte Brontë

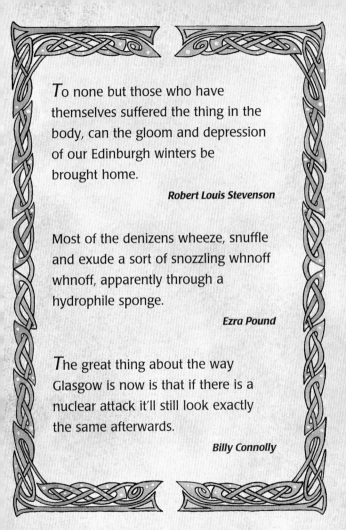

*T*o none but those who have themselves suffered the thing in the body, can the gloom and depression of our Edinburgh winters be brought home.

Robert Louis Stevenson

Most of the denizens wheeze, snuffle and exude a sort of snozzling whnoff whnoff, apparently through a hydrophile sponge.

Ezra Pound

*T*he great thing about the way Glasgow is now is that if there is a nuclear attack it'll still look exactly the same afterwards.

Billy Connolly

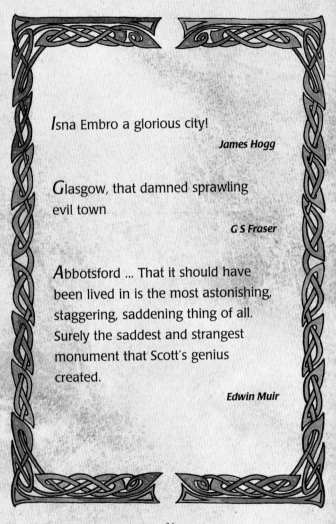

Isna Embro a glorious city!

James Hogg

Glasgow, that damned sprawling
evil town

G S Fraser

Abbotsford ... That it should have
been lived in is the most astonishing,
staggering, saddening thing of all.
Surely the saddest and strangest
monument that Scott's genius
created.

Edwin Muir

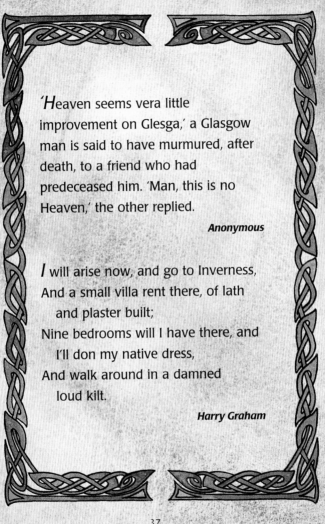

'Heaven seems vera little improvement on Glesga,' a Glasgow man is said to have murmured, after death, to a friend who had predeceased him. 'Man, this is no Heaven,' the other replied.

Anonymous

I will arise now, and go to Inverness,
And a small villa rent there, of lath
   and plaster built;
Nine bedrooms will I have there, and
   I'll don my native dress,
And walk around in a damned
   loud kilt.

Harry Graham

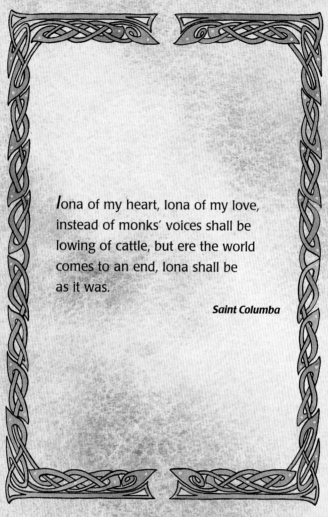

Iona of my heart, Iona of my love,
instead of monks' voices shall be
lowing of cattle, but ere the world
comes to an end, Iona shall be
as it was.

Saint Columba

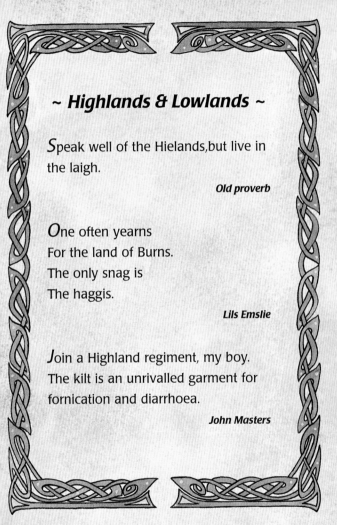

~ Highlands & Lowlands ~

*S*peak well of the Hielands, but live in the laigh.

Old proverb

*O*ne often yearns
For the land of Burns.
The only snag is
The haggis.

Lils Emslie

*J*oin a Highland regiment, my boy.
The kilt is an unrivalled garment for
fornication and diarrhoea.

John Masters

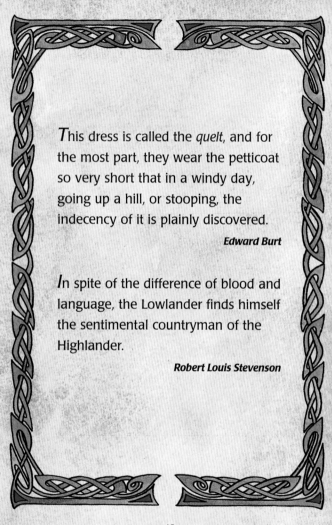

*T*his dress is called the *quelt*, and for the most part, they wear the petticoat so very short that in a windy day, going up a hill, or stooping, the indecency of it is plainly discovered.

Edward Burt

*I*n spite of the difference of blood and language, the Lowlander finds himself the sentimental countryman of the Highlander.

Robert Louis Stevenson

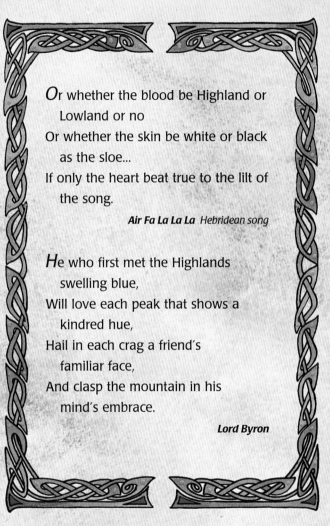

*O*r whether the blood be Highland or
Lowland or no
Or whether the skin be white or black
as the sloe...
If only the heart beat true to the lilt of
the song.

Air Fa La La La *Hebridean song*

*H*e who first met the Highlands
swelling blue,
Will love each peak that shows a
kindred hue,
Hail in each crag a friend's
familiar face,
And clasp the mountain in his
mind's embrace.

Lord Byron

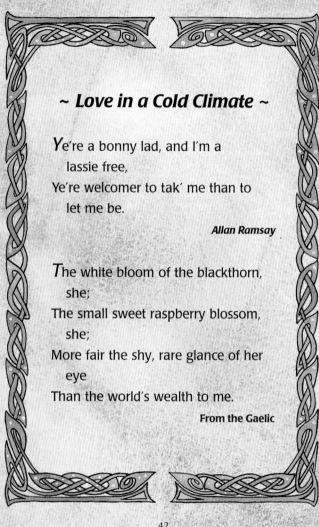

~ *Love in a Cold Climate* ~

*Y*e're a bonny lad, and I'm a
  lassie free,
Ye're welcomer to tak' me than to
  let me be.

Allan Ramsay

*T*he white bloom of the blackthorn,
  she;
The small sweet raspberry blossom,
  she;
More fair the shy, rare glance of her
  eye
Than the world's wealth to me.

From the Gaelic

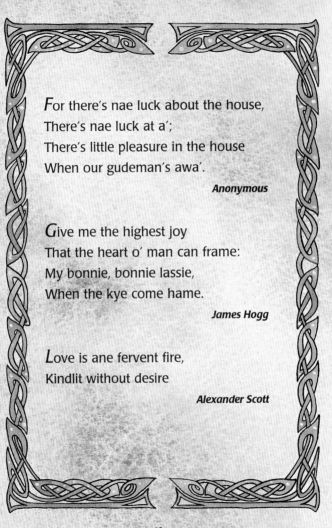

For there's nae luck about the house,
There's nae luck at a';
There's little pleasure in the house
When our gudeman's awa'.

Anonymous

Give me the highest joy
That the heart o' man can frame:
My bonnie, bonnie lassie,
When the kye come hame.

James Hogg

Love is ane fervent fire,
Kindlit without desire

Alexander Scott

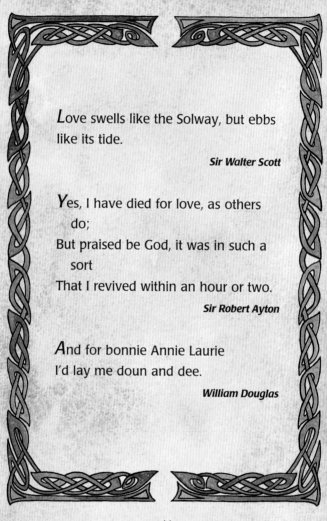

*L*ove swells like the Solway, but ebbs like its tide.

Sir Walter Scott

*Y*es, I have died for love, as others do;
But praised be God, it was in such a sort
That I revived within an hour or two.

Sir Robert Ayton

*A*nd for bonnie Annie Laurie
I'd lay me doun and dee.

William Douglas

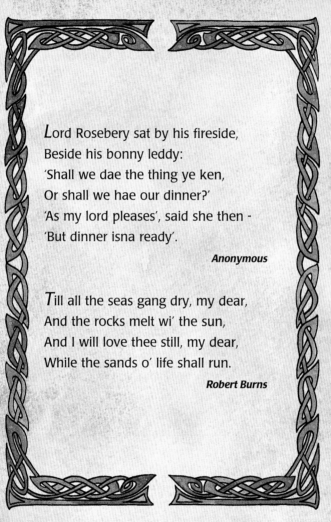

Lord Rosebery sat by his fireside,
Beside his bonny leddy:
'Shall we dae the thing ye ken,
Or shall we hae our dinner?'
'As my lord pleases', said she then -
'But dinner isna ready'.

Anonymous

Till all the seas gang dry, my dear,
And the rocks melt wi' the sun,
And I will love thee still, my dear,
While the sands o' life shall run.

Robert Burns

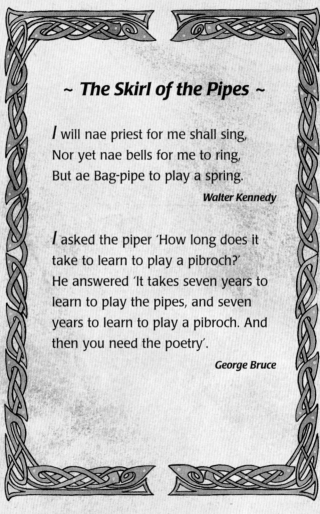

~ *The Skirl of the Pipes* ~

I will nae priest for me shall sing,
Nor yet nae bells for me to ring,
But ae Bag-pipe to play a spring.

Walter Kennedy

I asked the piper 'How long does it
take to learn to play a pibroch?'
He answered 'It takes seven years to
learn to play the pipes, and seven
years to learn to play a pibroch. And
then you need the poetry'.

George Bruce

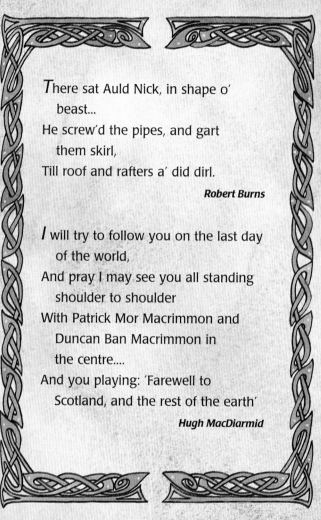

There sat Auld Nick, in shape o'
   beast...
He screw'd the pipes, and gart
   them skirl,
Till roof and rafters a' did dirl.

Robert Burns

I will try to follow you on the last day
   of the world,
And pray I may see you all standing
   shoulder to shoulder
With Patrick Mor Macrimmon and
   Duncan Ban Macrimmon in
   the centre....
And you playing: 'Farewell to
   Scotland, and the rest of the earth'

Hugh MacDiarmid

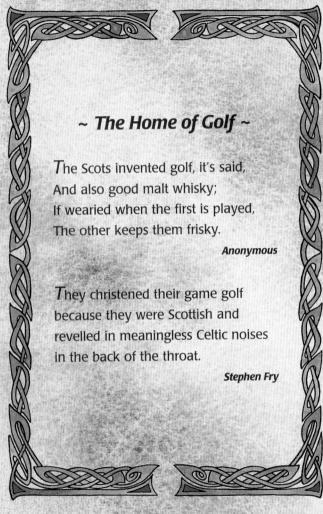

~ *The Home of Golf* ~

The Scots invented golf, it's said,
And also good malt whisky;
If wearied when the first is played,
The other keeps them frisky.

Anonymous

They christened their game golf
because they were Scottish and
revelled in meaningless Celtic noises
in the back of the throat.

Stephen Fry

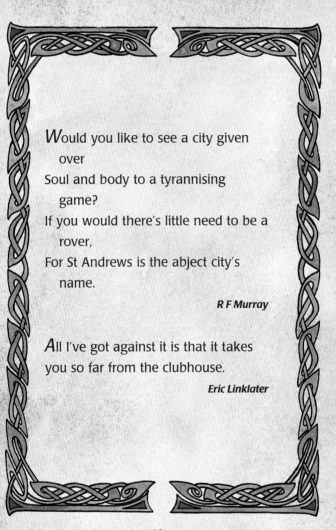

Would you like to see a city given over
  over
Soul and body to a tyrannising
  game?
If you would there's little need to be a
  rover,
For St Andrews is the abject city's
  name.

R F Murray

All I've got against it is that it takes
you so far from the clubhouse.

Eric Linklater

49

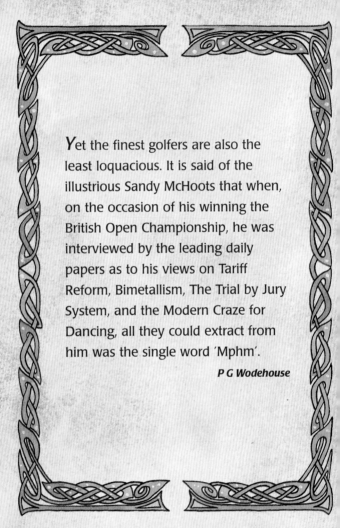

*Y*et the finest golfers are also the least loquacious. It is said of the illustrious Sandy McHoots that when, on the occasion of his winning the British Open Championship, he was interviewed by the leading daily papers as to his views on Tariff Reform, Bimetallism, The Trial by Jury System, and the Modern Craze for Dancing, all they could extract from him was the single word 'Mphm'.

P G Wodehouse

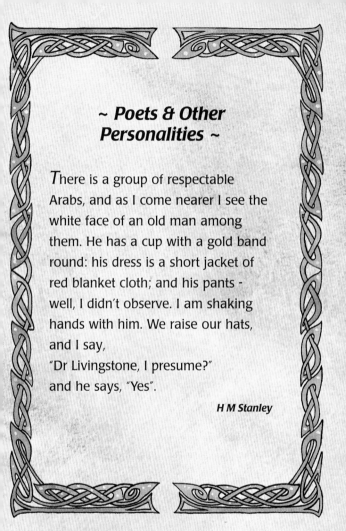

~ *Poets & Other Personalities* ~

There is a group of respectable Arabs, and as I come nearer I see the white face of an old man among them. He has a cup with a gold band round: his dress is a short jacket of red blanket cloth; and his pants - well, I didn't observe. I am shaking hands with him. We raise our hats, and I say,

"Dr Livingstone, I presume?"
and he says, "Yes".

H M Stanley

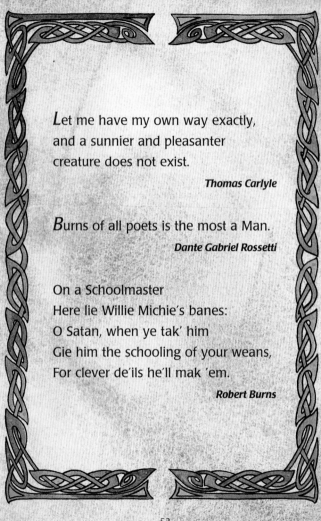

*L*et me have my own way exactly,
and a sunnier and pleasanter
creature does not exist.

Thomas Carlyle

*B*urns of all poets is the most a Man.

Dante Gabriel Rossetti

On a Schoolmaster
Here lie Willie Michie's banes:
O Satan, when ye tak' him
Gie him the schooling of your weans,
For clever de'ils he'll mak 'em.

Robert Burns

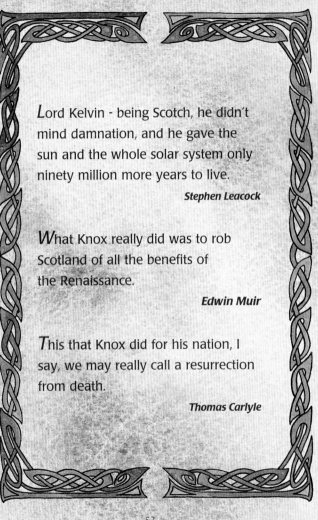

Lord Kelvin - being Scotch, he didn't mind damnation, and he gave the sun and the whole solar system only ninety million more years to live.

Stephen Leacock

What Knox really did was to rob Scotland of all the benefits of the Renaissance.

Edwin Muir

This that Knox did for his nation, I say, we may really call a resurrection from death.

Thomas Carlyle

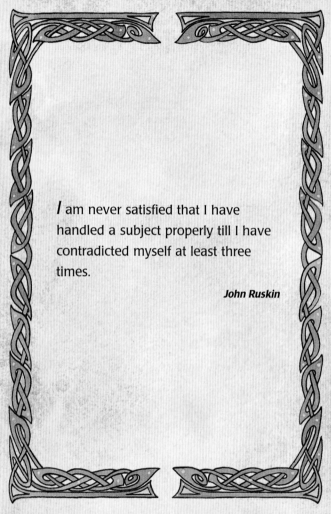

I am never satisfied that I have handled a subject properly till I have contradicted myself at least three times.

John Ruskin

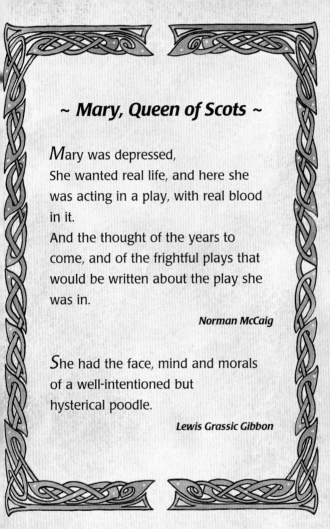

~ *Mary, Queen of Scots* ~

*M*ary was depressed,
She wanted real life, and here she
was acting in a play, with real blood
in it.
And the thought of the years to
come, and of the frightful plays that
would be written about the play she
was in.

Norman McCaig

*S*he had the face, mind and morals
of a well-intentioned but
hysterical poodle.

Lewis Grassic Gibbon

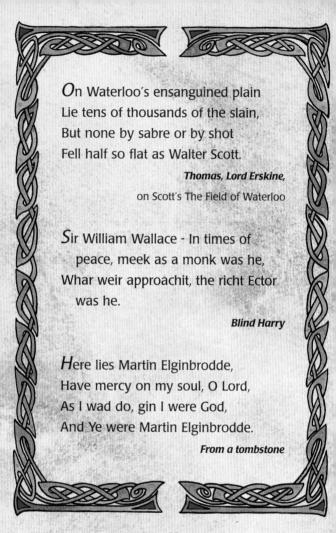

*O*n Waterloo's ensanguined plain
Lie tens of thousands of the slain,
But none by sabre or by shot
Fell half so flat as Walter Scott.

Thomas, Lord Erskine,
on Scott's The Field of Waterloo

*S*ir William Wallace - In times of
   peace, meek as a monk was he,
Whar weir approachit, the richt Ector
   was he.

Blind Harry

*H*ere lies Martin Elginbrodde,
Have mercy on my soul, O Lord,
As I wad do, gin I were God,
And Ye were Martin Elginbrodde.

From a tombstone

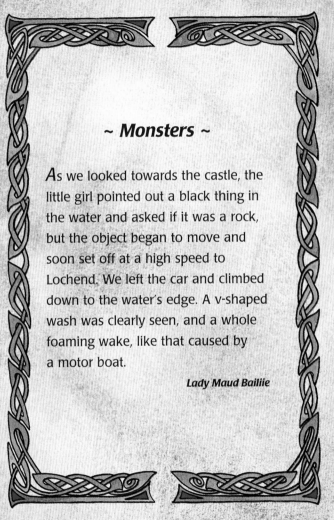

~ *Monsters* ~

*A*s we looked towards the castle, the little girl pointed out a black thing in the water and asked if it was a rock, but the object began to move and soon set off at a high speed to Lochend. We left the car and climbed down to the water's edge. A v-shaped wash was clearly seen, and a whole foaming wake, like that caused by a motor boat.

Lady Maud Bailiie

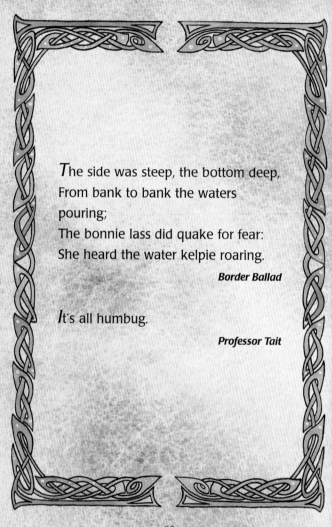

*T*he side was steep, the bottom deep,
From bank to bank the waters pouring;
The bonnie lass did quake for fear:
She heard the water kelpie roaring.

Border Ballad

*I*t's all humbug.

Professor Tait